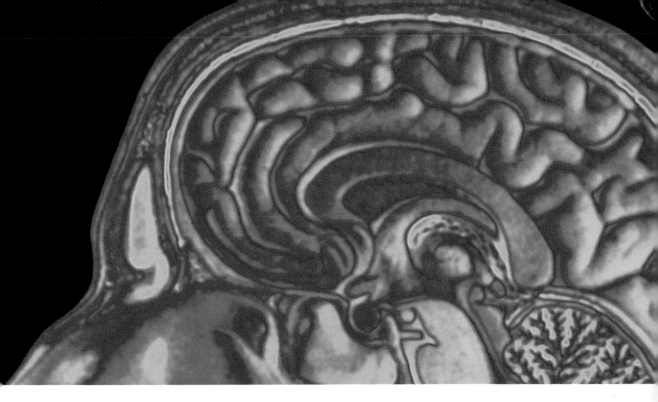

CUTTING EDGE MEDICINE

Seeing Inside the Body

Andrew Solway

WORLD ALMANAC® LIBRARY

Please visit our Web site at: **www.garethstevens.com**
For a free color catalog describing World Almanac® Library's list of high-quality books
and multimedia programs, call 1-800-848-2928 (USA) or 1-800-387-3178 (Canada).
World Almanac® Library's fax: (414) 332-3567.

Library of Congress Cataloging-in-Publication Data available upon request from publisher.
Fax (414) 336-0157 for the attention of the Publishing Records Department.

ISBN 978-0-8368-7869-1 (lib. bdg.)

This North American edition first published in 2007 by
World Almanac® Library
A Member of the WRC Media Family of Companies
330 West Olive Street, Suite 100
Milwaukee, WI 53212 USA

Produced by Arcturus Publishing Limited.
Editor: Alex Woolf
Designer: Nick Phipps
Consultant: Dr. Eleanor Clarke

World Almanac® Library editor: Carol Ryback
World Almanac® Library designer: Kami M. Strunsee
World Almanac® Library art direction: Tammy West
World Almanac® Library production: Jessica Yanke and Robert Kraus

The right of Andrew Solway to be identified as the author of this work has been
asserted by him in accordance with the Copyright, Designs and Patents Act, 1988.

Photo credits: Science Photo Library: / Mehau Kulyk 5; / Andrew Lambert Photography 7; / Gusto 9, 10, 13; / Mauro
Fermariello 15; /, ISM / Sovereign 16, 48; / ISM / Dr. M.O. Habert, Pitié-Salpatiere; / Wellcome Dept. of Cognitive Neurology
20; / CC Studio 22; / Alfred Pasieka cover, 25; / Simon Fraser 26; / Arthur Toga/UCLA 29; / Victor Habbick Visions 31;
/ Saturn Stills 33; / Dr. Najeeb Layyous 34; / CNRI 36; / Zephyr 39; / David M. Martin, M.D. 40; / Princess Margaret Rose
Orthopaedic Hospital 43; / James King-Holmes 44; / ISM 47; / Sam Ogden 51; / MIT AI Lab/Surgical Planning Lab/
Brigham & Women's Hospital 53; / University of Durham/Simon Fraser 55; / David Parker 57; Erik Viktor 58.

Printed in China

1 2 3 4 5 6 7 8 9 10 10 09 08 07 06

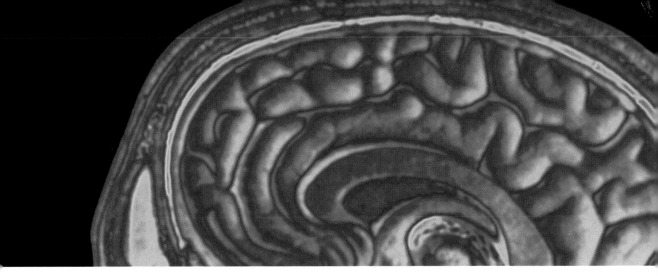

Contents

YA
616. 0754
SO 48

CHAPTER 1

What Is Medical Imaging?

On October 1, 1971, a small hospital in London, England, tested a strange-looking machine. It was a large, gleaming white box structure with a circular hole in it, big enough for a patient's head. A woman was lying in front of the machine, with just her head in the hole. As the machine hummed and whirred, an anxious group of people watched a TV monitor. After several minutes, a black-and-white picture formed, showing a cross-section through the patient's brain. The watchers pointed excitedly at the screen and began to clap and cheer.

CUTTING EDGE   SCIENCE

Why do we need to see inside the body?

Proper diagnosis of a patient's illness is one of the most challenging and important aspects facing physicians. Diagnosis is the process of determining what is wrong with a patient. Before the development of X-rays and medical imaging, doctors had two main methods for reaching a diagnosis: They asked patients to describe their symptoms, and they conducted a clinical examination—observing, touching, and listening to the patient's body in order to discover the problem.

While these methods remain important, they are not always reliable because the body is highly complex and the symptoms of illnesses are often similar. The ability to see inside the body has equipped doctors with a third method of diagnosing illnesses, one that can pinpoint the source and location of a problem with an accuracy that was not previously possible. As we shall discover in this book, the advances in medical imaging have transformed medicine and greatly improved the treatment of illnesses such as cancer, stroke, epilepsy, multiple sclerosis, and many others.

The first scanner

The test on this woman marked the first time a hospital used the CT (computed tomography) scanner. A CT scans a body with X-rays (*see page 7*) to form an image (previously called a "CAT scan"). The CT scanner was the first of several new types of scanners that have revolutionized medicine since the 1970s. Using scanners to make pictures of the inside of the body is known as medical imaging. To learn more about CT scanners, see Chapter 3.

The first medical test of a scanner was a great success. The images taken by the CT scanner showed a dark, circular shape in the front part of the brain. This indicated the location of a cyst—an abnormal sac containing fluid. After the operation to remove the cyst, the surgeon remarked that the cyst looked "exactly like the picture!"

Tools for diagnosis

Medical imaging has given doctors a set of powerful new tools for diagnosing a patient's problems. Modern scanners can create excellent pictures of the body's internal organs (such as the liver, stomach, and heart). Some scanners can create 3-D pictures, while others highlight a particular type of problem, such as a tumor (an abnormal growth or mass of cells). The story of scanners began in the late nineteenth century, with the discovery of X-rays.

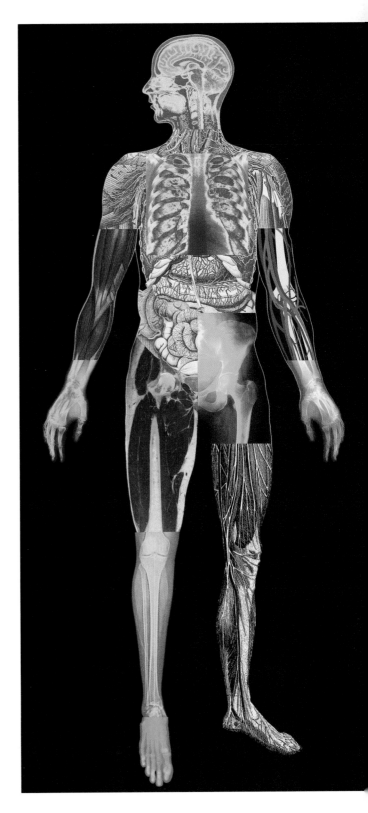

This image of the human body was made using several types of imaging, including an MRI scan (the head) and an X-ray (the pelvis).

CHAPTER 2

X-rays

In November 1895, German physics professor Wilhelm Röentgen was experimenting in his laboratory with a cathode ray tube. A cathode ray tube is just another name for the main tube of a traditional television (not the thin, flat-screened kind). Röentgen's instrument consisted of a sealed glass tube with all the air pumped out of it. Two wires running from the tube were connected to a powerful battery.

Röentgen was using the cathode ray tube (CRT) in the dark and noticed that a screen covered with fluorescent material elsewhere in the room was shining brightly. (A fluorescent material glows, or fluoresces, when light or some other kind of energy hits it.) Röentgen knew that the cathode rays (*see sidebar, below*) were not making the screen fluoresce. Cathode rays cannot travel more than a few inches (centimeters) through air. He realized that the CRT was producing some other kind of invisible radiation. Radiation is energy that travels in the form of waves or rays. Röentgen called this new, unknown radiation "X-rays."

CUTTING EDGE   SCIENCE

Cathode ray tubes

Scientists experimenting with electricity tried pumping all the air out of a glass tube in order to see whether electricity could travel through the vacuum (empty space) inside the tube. They found that when the electricity passed through a vacuum, it produced "cathode rays," which traveled in a straight line from the cathode (negative end) of the tube to the anode (the positive end). Today, cathode ray tubes are used in traditional television sets and bulky computer monitors.

An accidental discovery

Röentgen placed various materials between the CRT and the fluorescent screen to learn more about the new rays. At some point, Röentgen accidentally put his hand between the CRT and the screen. The image he saw barely showed the soft parts of his hand, but the rays made a spooky image of the bones in his hand on the screen. Röentgen had unwittingly made the first X-ray image.

What are X-rays?

We now know that X-rays are part of the electromagnetic spectrum. Just as light rays spread out from the source in waves, X-rays also spread out like ripples in a pond. Waves from the electromagnetic spectrum are pure energy, however, so they travel much farther

Cathode rays in a cathode ray tube cause the tube to glow when they hit the glass. In this tube, a cross, hung between the cathode and the anode, blocks some of the cathode rays and produces a shadow on the glass.

than water waves. A wide range of different types of radiation make up the electromagnetic spectrum. Although they all have different frequencies (energy levels), they all travel at the same speed—the speed of light. Lower-energy waves such as infrared, microwaves, and radio waves are at one end of the spectrum, visible light is near the middle, and high-energy X-rays are at the other end.

Because of their high energy, X-rays can pass through many materials that light cannot pass through. Bones, however, are thick and dense enough to block X-rays. For a medical X-ray, the X-rays are shone through the body and made into a digital image. In the past, hospitals used photographic film to create an X-ray image, but digital images are much faster and cheaper to produce. (*See page 13 for more information.*) X-rays cannot pass through a patient's

CUTTING EDGE — SCIENTISTS

Wilhelm Röentgen (1845–1923)

Wilhelm Röentgen was born in Lennep, Germany, but his family moved to the Netherlands when he was three. Röentgen was not a particularly eager student, although he loved natural history. He spent much time roaming the countryside and was also very good at making machines. In 1869, he received his Ph.D. in physics from the University of Utrecht in the Netherlands. Röentgen was a lecturer and later a professor at several universities before moving to Würtzburg, Germany, where he made his X-ray discoveries. In 1901, he was awarded the first Nobel Prize in Physics for his work on X-rays.

bones, so the bones form a "shadowy" image. The bones usually show up as light shadows against a dark background.

Spreading like wildfire

Röentgen discovered that the X-rays caused photographic film to blacken, and he made use of this property to create the first X-ray pictures. Röentgen's report on X-rays was published in December 1895. Newspapers and magazines quickly picked up the sensational story. Many scientists were experimenting with CRTs similar to Röentgen's, and within weeks they were also producing X-ray images. Doctors immediately saw how useful X-rays were in their own profession. In February 1896, less than two months after Röentgen's discovery was made public, Edwin Frost, a doctor at Dartmouth College in Hanover, New Hampshire, produced an X-ray image that was used to diagnose a broken wrist.

The first X-rays were taken on photographic film, but by March 1896, Thomas Edison had developed an instrument called a fluoroscope. It showed X-ray pictures in "real time" as moving images on a fluorescent screen. Investigating the body using moving, real-time X-ray pictures is called fluoroscopy.

At first, X-rays could only make a person's bones visible. Later, in the 1920s, researchers found that by injecting special dyes into a person's bloodstream, they could also make blood vessels show up on an X-ray. This use of X-rays became known as angiography (*see pages 12–13 and 36–37*).

Dangerous rays

High-energy radiation like X-rays can be harmful. Several hours' exposure to X-rays can cause injuries, such as skin burns and hair

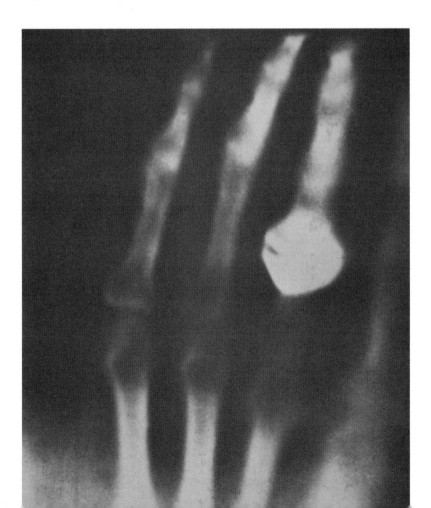

Röentgen's scientific paper included this X-ray picture of his wife's hand. It was one of the first X-rays ever taken. The bones of Anna Röentgen's hand and the ring on her finger are clearly visible.

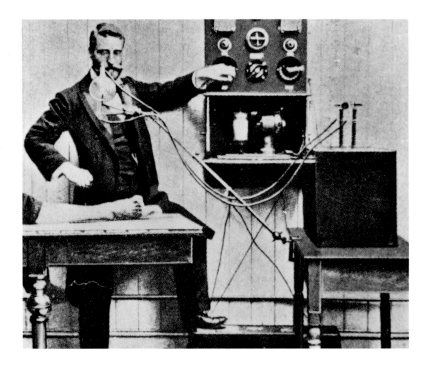

This early portable X-ray machine was designed for military use. The man using it, Ernest Harnack, worked at the London Hospital in England. Like Clarence Dally (*see text*), Harnack suffered injuries from X-ray exposure and eventually died of cancer.

loss within a few hours or days. Exposure to smaller doses of X-rays over a longer period also causes damage. Such damage can take several years to appear, and it often causes cancer.

The dangers of X-rays were not immediately recognized, and people used X-rays in many ways that were unsafe. Physicist Nikolai Tesla warned experimenters in 1896 that they "should not get too close to the X-ray tube," but his warning was often ignored. In 1904, Clarence Dally, Thomas Edison's chief X-ray researcher, died from cancers caused by excessive exposure to X-rays. Many other early researchers also became ill or died because of damage caused by X-rays. Radiologists and radiologic technologists (doctors who specialize in X-rays and the people who produce the X-rays, respectively) wear "badges" that measure their exposure to X-rays.

The X-ray craze

Although the injuries and illnesses of X-ray researchers and patients showed that X-rays could be dangerous, this did not stop the widespread use of X-ray machines, sometimes for trivial purposes. Some cities in the U.S. had X-ray machines that allowed people to look at the bones in their hands. As late as the 1940s, shoe stores often had "Foot-o-Scope" machines that showed foot bones.

Improvements in X-rays

Although fluoroscopes showed an immediate image, early X-ray machines required X-ray exposure times of up to two hours to get a good picture on film. X-ray machines were improved in the early twentieth century, and by 1906, the required exposure time was no more than a few seconds. The reduction in the amount of radiation absorbed by the patient made getting an X-ray much safer.

Other improvements produced much clearer, brighter X-ray pictures. In 1913, German physician Gustav Bucky found that he could get rid of "stray" X-rays that caused blurring and "snow" on X-ray pictures. He put metal grids in front of the X-ray tube and between the patient and the film. U.S. inventer Hollis Potter improved this practice by moving the grids slowly while the X-ray was taken. The moving grids improved the image, and their shadows did not appear on the final X-ray image.

Safety regulations

Although a patient getting an X-ray no longer got burned by the procedure, prolonged exposure to the rays could still cause problems such as cancer later in life. The long-term effects of X-rays only gradually became clear. By the 1930s, however, scientists had plenty of evidence that X-rays were harmful in high doses. In 1931, X-ray experts introduced a maximum X-ray dosage limit beyond which they believed X-rays were harmful.

German physicist Otto Glasser developed a method for measuring radiation exposure that made it safer for those who

CUTTING EDGE MOMENTS

X-rays in court

Almost as soon as they were discovered, X-rays proved useful in court cases. During Christmas 1895, George Holder shot fellow Canadian Tolman Cunnings in the leg in a Montreal bar. Doctors could not find the bullet. In 1896, Cunnings took Holder to court. Holder's lawyers said that Holder had not shot Cunnings and there was no bullet to prove that he had. Cunnings then had his leg X-rayed and the resulting image showed the bullet lodged there. Doctors removed the bullet, and this—together with the X-ray picture—was enough to convict Holder.

worked with radiation equipment. Workers began wearing badges made of photographic film that turned black when exposed to too much X-ray radiation. People who work with X-rays today still wear a similar type of detector.

Development of X-rays

By 1905, X-rays were being widely used as a medical tool. Doctors used them to look at bones if they suspected a fracture (break). Chest X-rays helped identify pneumonia, lung cancer, and edema (fluid in the lungs).

X-ray fluoroscopes proved useful for on-the-spot examinations, but for good-quality images and a permanent record, an X-ray picture was best. Taking large numbers of X-ray pictures was slow work until 1946, when George Schoenander developed an automatic film cassette that could take X-rays at a rate of 1.5 per second. By 1953, the film cassette could take six pictures per second.

CUTTING EDGE   FACTS

The pros and cons of X-rays

The main advantages of X-rays are their widespread availability and relative cheapness compared to other kinds of scan. Also, it is possible to take many X-ray images per second to show a "movie" of the area of interest. The main disadvantages of X-rays are that they do not show most of the body's soft tissues (muscles and organs, for example), and they only show a two-dimensional (flat) view—usually in black and white (although X-rays can now be artificially colored).

X-ray TV

As X-ray machines improved, it became possible to obtain a good image using much smaller doses of X-rays. In 1955, another invention called the image intensifier made it possible to use smaller doses of X-rays when using a fluoroscope. The image intensifier amplified (made stronger and clearer) the fluoroscope images. The amplified images could be displayed on a TV screen. By the 1960s, this "X-ray TV" had replaced the fluoroscope.

With an image intensifier, angiography (the injecting of dyes into a patient's bloodstream to make the blood vessels show up on an

X-ray) became a much more useful tool. Angiography is often used to find problems with blood flow in any part of the body, especially in the cardiac (heart) vessels.

Digital X-rays

Until recently, all X-ray images were produced by shining X-rays onto photographic film. This changed in 2000, when digital X-ray machines became available. Digital X-ray machines form an image using numeric codes. For a digital X-ray, the X-rays are shone through the body onto an array of thousands of digital detectors. Each detector records a number that stands for the amount of X-rays that hit it. A computer combines all the numbers from the detectors to form a digital image—which is also stored on a computer.

Digital X-rays have many advantages over traditional X-rays. They "develop" instantly, so no messy chemicals or dark room is necessary to produce them. Doctors can view the X-rays on a screen or as a printout and can send images instantaneously to different hospitals for another doctor's opinion. The X-rays can also be stored on a compact disk as a permanent medical record.

A modern X-ray room. Compared to the early X-ray machine shown on page 10, modern X-ray machines are far quicker, produce better images, and using much less radiation than earlier technology.

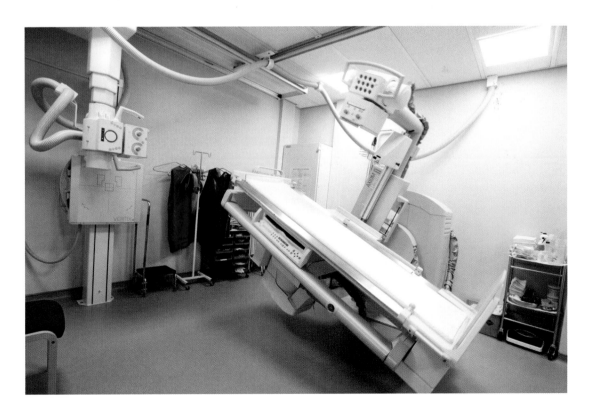

CHAPTER 3

Computer-aided Imaging

Bones and teeth show up on X-ray pictures because they absorb X-rays (they do not allow them to pass through). By contrast, the body's soft tissues hardly show up on X-ray pictures because most X-rays pass through them. The soft tissues are not completely transparent, however. An X-ray usually shows a "ghost" image of the soft tissues because the soft tissues absorb a small amount of X-rays. In the 1960s, scientists worked on ways of using this partial absorption by the soft tissues to produce more complete images of the inside of the body.

The computed tomography (CT) scanner

In 1967, English engineer Godfrey Hounsfield was developing an X-ray machine that could take photographs of soft body tissues from many different angles. The soft tissues would absorb X-rays according to their depth and thickness and the particular angle at which the X-ray was taken. A computer could use data to compose an image that looked like a slice through the body. The resulting images would give a sense of the depth and position of internal structures, including its soft tissues, that was not possible with a conventional X-ray.

Hounsfield called his machine a computed tomography (CT)

CUTTING EDGE — SCIENCE

How CT works

In a normal X-ray, the rays produced by an X-ray tube travel through the patient and fall on a piece of photographic film, a fluorescent screen, or digitized receptors. In a CT scanner, the X-ray tube is circular and positioned opposite an array of detectors. The patient lies in the center of the ring. The X-ray tube and the detectors move in a circle around his or her body, taking many X-ray photographs as they go around. The detectors record X-rays as they pass through the body at a wide range of different angles. A computer combines the digital images to create pictures of cross-sectional slices through the body.

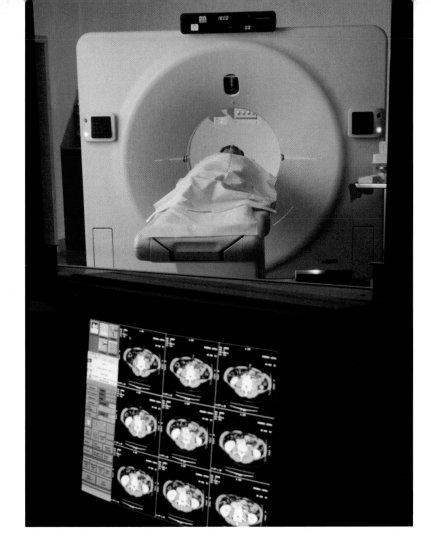

A patient undergoing a CT scan. The monitor in the foreground shows pictures of some of the body "slices" taken by the scanner.

scanner. "Computed" refers to the fact that the machine used a computer to help create its images. "Tomography" is Greek for "a picture of a plane." It means that the CT scanner makes images of cross-sectional "slices" through the body. The CT scanner produces its images using a moving X-ray tube, a group of detectors, and a computer (*see sidebar, page 14*).

Most people first heard of CT scans as "CAT" scans—for "computed axial tomography." Medical facilities and personnel now prefer the term "CT." The first CT scanners were used only for brain scans, but by 1976, whole-body-sized scanners were developed. Hounsfield's first scanner took several hours to collect the information needed for a single "slice" through the body, and the computer took days to construct an image. Early scanners used in hospitals produced an image of a single slice in about four minutes. Today's CT scanners take less than a second to produce an image—and development of even faster scanners is underway.

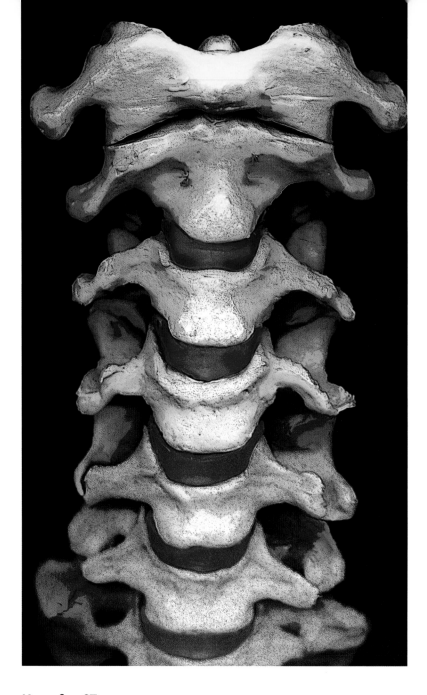

This picture of cervical (neck) bones (vertebrae) may look artificial, but it is an actual 3-D CT scan. (*See page 17 for more details.*) The white areas are bone, and the reddish sections are disks of cartilage (tough, flexible connective tissue) that cushion the vertebrae.

Uses for CT

It quickly became clear that CT scanners could see inside the body far more clearly than ordinary X-rays. The first CT machines were used mostly to scan a brain and pinpoint the position of a cancerous tumor before surgery. As CT scanner technology has improved, the scanners have been used to help diagnose many other problems. They are used to locate tumors in other parts of the body, especially in the lungs, liver, and intestines. CT scans are also useful for revealing the damage caused by head injuries and for detecting bleeding in the brain. CT is the best technique for diagnosing problems in the chest and lungs because it provides some of the best images of these areas.

CT improvements

CT scanners have improved in many ways since the 1970s. Faster computers and improved software mean that scanners can produce much better images more quickly and in more detail. Thirty years ago, a CT scanner produced one black-and-white image of a single body "slice" in about four minutes. Today's scanners produce a far superior image to that in merely half a second. Computers can also be programmed to color the images so that blood vessels or other details stand out more clearly.

Three-dimensionsal (3-D) images

The most important advance in CT scanners is their ability to produce three-dimensional (3-D) images of different parts of the body on a computer screen. Conventional X-rays are two-dimensional (2-D) images. The CT's computer takes the 2-D "slices" and puts them together to make a "virtual" 3-D model of the region being scanned. The radiologist still views a 2-D image, but he or she can manipulate that image many different ways. For instance, the radiologist can strip away the skin and muscle to inspect the internal organs, view slices through the body from many different angles, or highlight particular structures—such as tumors or blood vessels—with bright colors.

CUTTING EDGE   FACTS

Whole-body CT scans

Today's CT scanners can quickly take images of the whole body. This technology is very useful in the emergency room. An emergency room patient with serious injuries can undergo a whole-body CT scan, enabling doctors to almost instantly identify major internal injuries.

Some people have begun to have whole-body CT scans simply as a "baseline" record of their health. A 2004 study, however, showed that baseline scans can themselves pose a health risk. Although modern scanners use low-dose X-rays, a patient undergoing a whole-body CT scan is exposed to an overall large dose of X-rays. A single whole-body CT scan once in a person's lifetime probably is not harmful, but repeated whole-body scans significantly increases one's cancer risk later in life.

CHAPTER 4

Harnessing Radioactivity

The CT scanner was not the first medical scanner to be developed. Researchers had been trying for years to create pictures of the body using radioactive materials or radiation other than X-rays. A radioactive material is one that naturally gives off some form of radiation. An instrument called a Geiger counter can detect radioactivity.

Early radioactive studies

The property of radioactivity was discovered in 1896, a year after the discovery of X-rays. Researchers realized that if they could make radioactive versions of natural substances and inject them into the body, the radioactivity would act as a "tag" or "label" that would make it possible to track its course through the body. A patient's bloodstream would serve as the natural carrier for distributing the radioactive element around the body. Researchers could then create an image of where the radioactive elements ended up.

In the 1930s, scientists managed to produce radioactive versions —radioisotopes—of elements such as oxygen and hydrogen. Researchers injected the "tagged" elements into the body and tracked them using a Geiger counter or other detector. At that time, no one knew if radioisotopes were safe. Hungarian physicist George de Hevesy felt that the only way to test the safety of radioisotopes was to experiment with them on himself!

SPECT

Early experiments with radioactive tagging were not designed to produce images of the inside of the body. By 1963, however, U.S. medical researchers David Edwards and Roy Kuhl had developed a radioactive tagging technique called SPECT (Single Photon

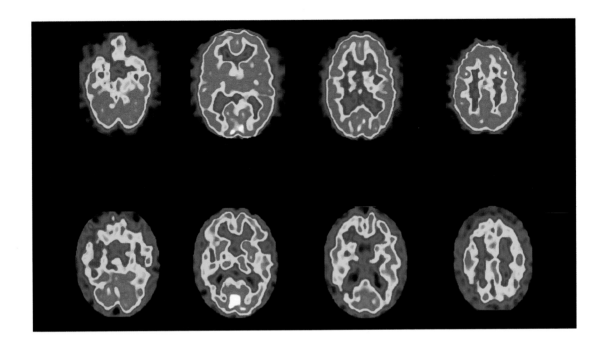

Emission Computed Tomography) that produces internal images of the body. A photon is an incredibly small particle of light or other radiative energy. SPECT uses radiation-sensitive cameras that rotate around the patient's body and produce images by detecting the photons emitted (given off) from the tagged substance.

SPECT imaging does not show body structures, as in an X-ray. Instead, it shows the distribution of the tagged substance. One substance that researchers commonly tag is glucose. Glucose is what the body's cells use for "food." Cells that are using a lot of energy (usually ones that are growing and dividing) take up a lot of glucose. Cancer cells grow and divide constantly, so a tumor takes up large amounts of glucose. This activity shows up as a concentration of radioactivity on a SPECT scan.

These SPECT scans show several cross sections through the brain, as seen from the top of the head. The top row shows a normal brain. The lower row shows the brain of someone with Alzheimer's disease. Red areas are the most active, while the least-active areas are dark blue. There is less activity in the brain of the Alzheimer's sufferer.

CUTTING EDGE   FACTS

SPECT
SPECT images are fairly crude, because instead of showing body structures, they show the distribution of a radioactive substance within the body. Because SPECT scanners are fairly cheap and simple to use, however, this type of scan continues to be widely used.

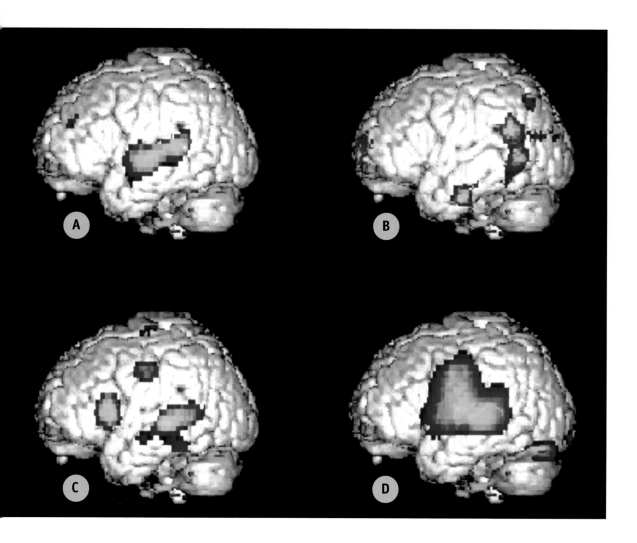

Positron emission tomography

Researchers who had been working to improve SPECT scanners realized combining the new imaging techniques would result in even better imaging technology. One team at the Washington University School of Medicine in St. Louis, Missouri, headed by Michel Ter-Pogossian, were working on a device using radioisotopes for imaging the brain. The device looked like a helmet covered in spikes. Ter-Pogossian's team incorporated some ideas from the CT scanner into their own device. The result was a hexagonally shaped machine that surrounded the patient and scanned the body for radioactivity from many different angles. As in CT scanning, a computer then combined the different scans to create an internal picture of the body.

These PET scans show brain activity when speaking or listening. Orange patches show which brain areas are active when (A) imagining speech, (B) comprehending spoken words, (C) repeating words, and (D) monitoring speech.

Ter-Pogossian's team named the new technique "positron emission tomography," or PET. It was called this because the radioisotopes used in a PET scanner emit incredibly small particles called positrons.

Until the 1980s, PET scanners were only used in research, and even today PET is more important in research than in diagnosing illness. This is because PET scanners need very skilled operators to work them, and the radioisotopes that they use are made in sophisticated machines that are usually only found in universities and other research facilities. PET scans have, however, proved very useful in diagnosing some brain problems (*see sidebar, below*).

How PET works

The radioisotope usually used in PET scans is a type of oxygen that gives off particles called positrons. The patient drinks a substance (usually glucose) that has been tagged with radioactive oxygen. (Many of the tagging substances can be used for various kinds of diagnostic tests that use different technologies.)

Radioisotopes that give off positrons are different from other radioactive materials because they give off two rays of radiation in exactly opposite directions. If two detectors on opposite sides of the PET scanner pick up a radioactive signal at the same time, it

CUTTING EDGE   MOMENTS

Half a brain

In 1985, two-year-old Ryan Peterson was brought to a brain clinic in Los Angeles, California. Ryan had suffered from seizures since he was born, but episodes suddenly began worsening. Other tests showed no problems in Ryan's brain, but a PET scan showed that the left half of Ryan's brain was not working properly. In 1986, surgeons removed the entire left half of Ryan's cerebral cortex (the outer part of the brain). Within a year, Ryan was talking and walking, and eventually he was able to attend school. Ryan's case showed clearly that PET scans are valuable for detecting brain disorders that other scans do not show. Ryan was one of the first people to benefit from a PET scan. Today, PET scans are regularly used to assess the problems of children with epilepsy. Most patients do not need such drastic brain surgery as that which Ryan had.

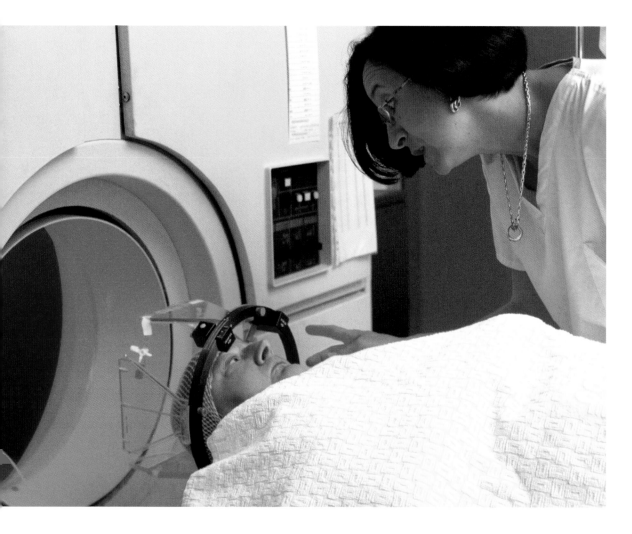

indicates that the radioactivity was given off somewhere between them. A computer uses that information to create an accurate record of where the tagged glucose ends up inside the body.

A nurse talks to a patient who is about to undergo a PET scan.

Advantages of PET

PET focuses on processes occurring in the body instead of showing body structures. For example, like SPECT, the PET scan also reveals cells that are using a lot of energy and dividing rapidly—but it shows these areas superimposed on a structural background of the body area. PET is, therefore, another useful tool for locating tumors.

PET scans are also used to measure nerve cell activity in the brain, which helps diagnose certain brain disorders. Radioactive water can also be used instead of glucose. The water is absorbed into the blood and shows up in the brain's blood supply. When nerve cells in part of the brain are working hard, blood flow to that area of the brain increases. A PET scan that reveals areas of increased blood flow therefore indicates increased nerve cell activity in the brain.

A PET scan can diagnose a brain-damaging illness, such as a stroke or epilepsy. For example, brain areas badly damaged by a stroke have no nerve cell activity and show up as black spots on the PET scan. Epilepsy can have similar symptoms to stroke, but the two illnesses cause different types of brain damage. A PET scan can detect these differences and distinguish between stroke victims and people with epilepsy.

Different tracers

Glucose is the most common tracer used in PET scans. Other kinds of tracers provide different kinds of information for a variety of suspected medical problems. For example, researchers have discovered that glucose is not a very helpful tracer for analyzing problems with the heart. Instead, a tracer made of a type of ammonia is tagged with substances such as radioactive rubidium or fluorine for cardiac PET scans. The normal blood flow pattern through the heart does not affect the information provided by the tracer material, so the doctors see a precise cardiac image. The cardiac PET scan produces a very accurate image of the heart's metabolism, and the tracer indicates areas of the heart that may be damaged.

CUTTING EDGE   FACTS

Problems with PET

The radioisotopes used for PET scans last only for a short time before losing their radioactivity, so they are produced on-site or close to the place where they are needed. Radioisotope production involves a complex machine called a cyclotron. Not all medical centers or hospital facilities have PET scanners.

Another disadvantage of PET scans is their use of radioactive materials. The idea of drinking a radioactive liquid makes some patients anxious. Also, although PET scans are considered safe for most patients, pregnant women should not undergo a PET scan. A developing fetus is especially sensitive to radioactivity and could be harmed by the PET scan procedure.

CHAPTER 5

Magnetic Resonance Imaging

Magnetic resonance imaging, or MRI, uses a combination of magnets and radio waves (the kind of waves that carry radio and TV broadcasts) to obtain information about the inside of the body. While CT and X-rays give the best images of bones and other dense tissues, MRI produces excellent images of any part of the body that contains water. The soft tissues of the body are full of water and show up very well on MRI scans.

Nuclear magnetic resonance

MRI developed out of a technique called NMR (nuclear magnetic resonance), which was developed in the 1950s. NMR was first used by chemists for analyzing chemical compounds (determining what atoms chemicals contain). NMR uses a combination of magnets and radio waves to identify the different kinds of atom in a compound.

In the 1960s, researchers found that NMR was also useful for looking at living tissues. In 1970, U.S. medical researcher Raymond Damadian, of the State University of New York in Brooklyn, began investigating tumor cells using NMR. He discovered that cancerous tissues produced different NMR signals from healthy tissues.

CUTTING EDGE — SCIENCE

How MRI works

MRI scanners work by detecting hydrogen atoms in the body. Hydrogen is a component of water, and since virtually all substances found in the human body contain water, there is not much that the MRI scanners cannot "see." One of the few body parts that MRI does not image well are bones, which are made mostly of calcium and contain little water. MRI scanners direct a combination of magnets and radio waves at the patient's body, causing the body's hydrogen atoms to send out very weak magnetic signals. Detectors in the MRI machine pick up these signals. Hydrogen atoms in different parts of the body give off very slightly different signals, depending on what other atoms are around them. A computer connected to the MRI machine analyzes the differences in the signals and constructs an image of internal body tissues.

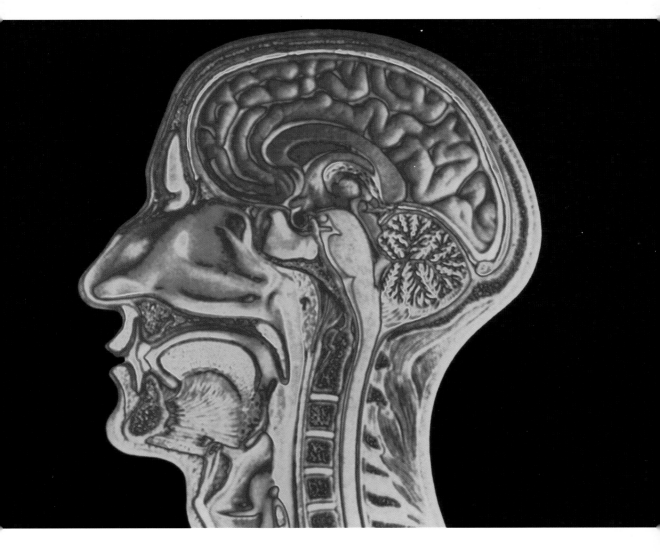

Damadian began working on a human-sized NMR machine that could be used to detect cancerous tumors in the body. He eventually unveiled his machine in 1977.

Although Damadian's machine was impressive, it was not yet an MRI scanner. The images it produced were very crude. Many other scientists put their efforts into the project before an MRI scanner that could compete with computed tomography was built. One of the most important contributions came from U.S. chemist Paul Lauterbur. He showed how to mathematically manipulate the information from an NMR machine to produce an image. By the early 1980s, ideas from a number of researchers had been combined to make the first practical MRI scanners.

As seen in this image of a head, MRI scans produce clear and detailed images of the internal body structures. The spine and spinal cord, the brain structures, the nasal cavity, the tongue, and the throat are all clearly visible in this scan.

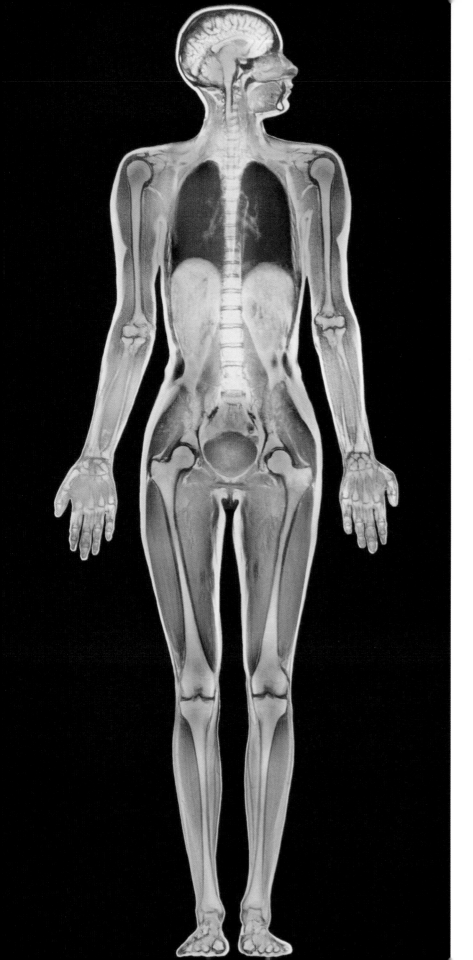

MRI scans were first used for making images of the brain, but they can also be used to make images of many other body parts.

Using MRI

By the mid-1980s, MRI scanners were beginning to appear in hospitals. Early MRI scanners could not produce images as clear as CT scanners. The machines were expensive, and it took a long time to obtain a good image. Despite those drawbacks, the MRI had advantages that many doctors found valuable. Even the early MRI scanners produced much better images of soft tissues than did CT scanners. MRI scans are especially good for showing soft tissues surrounded by bone or cartilage (rubbery connective tissues such as the ear or nose). In an MRI scan, bones become shadows, and the other tissues are shown in detail.

MRI is particularly useful in diagnosing tumors of the pituitary gland. The pituitary gland lies at the central base of the brain and is surrounded by skull bones. Only an MRI scan produces clear enough images to reveal a pituitary gland tumor.

Another early use of MRI was diagnosing multiple sclerosis (MS). In this disease, nerves in the brain and spinal cord become damaged when they lose the protective layer of fatty tissue (called a myelin sheath) that surrounds them. The symptoms of MS are quite variable, depending on how much nerve damage occurs. An MRI scan clearly shows this kind of nerve damage, allows doctors to confirm the diagnosis, and allows them to assess the severity of the disease. MRI has since become a powerful diagnostic tool. Globally, at least sixty million MRI procedures occur annually.

CUTTING EDGE   SCIENCE

MRI magnets

Patients who are scheduled for an MRI must avoid taking any magnetic objects into the scanner room. The magnets used in MRI scanners are immensely powerful. The main magnet can produce a magnetic field forty thousand times stronger than Earth's natural magnetic field. Items such as earrings, pens, hair clips, or any magnetic object inside the body, such as a pacemaker (an electrical device inserted into the body to keep the heart beating normally) or a blood vessel stent (a hollow metal mesh that props open a blood vessel), can be dangerous. In a few rare incidents, objects as large as oxygen tanks, refrigerators, and even a forklift truck were dragged across the room by the force of an in-use MRI magnet.

In the early days of MRI, some medical personnel worried that the strong magnetic fields inside the MRI machine might harm patients. MRI is no longer considered harmful and is instead regarded as safer than CT and PET—which rely on radiation that can be potentially harmful in large doses.

3-D MRI images

MRI scanners create 3-D images as well as flat "slices" through the body. The MRI images consist of data points called voxels (a combination of "volume" and "pixel") that represent a three-dimensional location. Doctors can rotate and "cut" in any direction a 3-D image created from voxels. This allows a surgeon to view an organ or a tumor from several different angles. The surgeon can better plan an operation by studying the MRI results.

Functional MRI

One newer form of MRI has greatly expanded its use in studies of how the brain works. In 1990, Japanese scientist Seiji Ogawa and colleagues showed that it was possible to use MRI to detect changes in blood flow within the brain. Using MRI this way is known as functional MRI, or fMRI.

When nerve cells are active, they use oxygen. Oxygen is carried to nerve cells in the blood, so a few seconds after nerve cells in an area of the brain become active, the blood flow to that part of the brain increases. Measuring the blood flow within the brain is therefore a fairly accurate guide to brain activity. So, like PET (*see pages 20–23*), fMRI is a powerful tool for mapping activity in different parts of the brain. The advantage of fMRI over PET is that fMRI machines do not need to be near facilities for

CUTTING EDGE   DEBATES

Does fMRI work?

Since its introduction in the 1990s, fMRI has been used in many studies to support a number of theories. For instance, there have been studies to show how coffee affects the brain, how women react to cartoons, and how commercials affect people watching sporting events. Many scientists criticize the conclusions drawn from these studies. They point out that it takes several seconds to produce each fMRI image, but brain activity patterns can change much more rapidly than this. Also, not all scientists agree with the idea that particular parts of the brain have specific jobs—they say other evidence suggests that brain function cannot be localized. Supporters of fMRI argue that these criticisms are problems with particular studies, not with the fMRI technique itself.

producing radioisotopes, and the images they produce are more detailed than PET images.

Scientists have used fMRI scans in many studies of brain activity. The brain of a subject is first scanned while the person is resting to get baseline data on brain activity. The subject is then given a simple activity to perform, for instance speaking, reading, picking up an object, or remembering a phrase. MRI scans are taken during the activity, and the results of the baseline scan are subtracted. What results is a series of images showing the areas of the brain that are most active during the activity.

As with CT scanners, modern MRI scanners can produce 3-D images of the brain and other body structures.

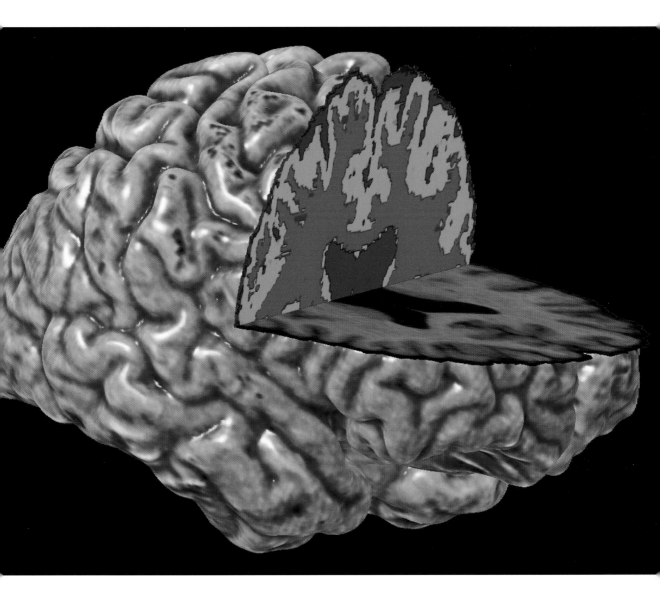

CHAPTER 6

Seeing With Sound

Doctors and researchers often use ultrasound (sound waves) to create images of the inside of the body. For example, at some point fairly early in a pregnancy, most women have an ultrasound scan of their fetus. Measurements taken of the fetus during an ultrasound help determine the delivery date and can indicate whether or not the fetus is developing normally. As the doctor or technician moves the ultrasound probe over the mother's abdomen, a TV monitor attached to the probe shows a blurry black-and-white image. When the probe finally focuses on the fetus, a tiny shape becomes apparent.

How ultrasound works

An ultrasound scanner sends pulses of extremely high-pitched sound—much higher frequencies than humans can hear—into the body. Like ordinary sound, ultrasound is made up of vibrations. Some vibrations pass through the body, but others bounce back from the organs, like echoes. Detectors inside the ultrasound probe pick up the high-pitched ultrasound echoes. The echoes from many

CUTTING EDGE   SCIENCE

What is ultrasound?

Ultrasound is sound frequencies beyond that of human hearing. The sounds are produced by piezoelectric crystals. These are special crystals that vibrate when a rapidly changing electric current (a flow of electricity) passes through them. Most state-of-the-art ultrasound equipment produces sounds that are three hundred times above the highest frequencies people can hear.

different pulses are processed by a computer, which uses the information to create an image.

The development of ultrasound

Researchers were using sound to look inside the body as early as 1937, when Austrian brothers Karl and Friedrich Dussik sent sound waves through the skull of a patient with a brain disease. The Dussiks' experiments had little success, however.

The invention of sonar (short for SOund NAvigation and Ranging) during World War II eventually led to the development of ultrasound technology. Warships used sonar to check water depth and to image the seabed. A sonar system sent sound pulses into the water and measured the echoes, which were detected by a special microphone. The time taken for the sound pulses to return measured the distance from the ship to objects below. Sonar helped the crew detect other ships, such as submarines, and helped the captain navigate around reefs or other underwater obstacles.

The ultrasound flaw detector, which revealed hidden cracks within pieces of metal, was another device developed during World War II. This detector checked metal vehicles, such as planes and tanks, for cracks that could weaken them. Many researchers at the time realized that something similar to the ultrasound flaw detector could also help create images of the inside of the body.

Bats navigate in the dark using an echolocation system that works like an ultrasound scanner. As shown in this computer-generated artwork, the bat sends out high-pitched bursts of ultrasound, and its ears detect the echoes of sound bouncing off objects around them. Bats "see" insects in flight using this echolocation system.

During the 1940s and 1950s, researchers took many different approaches to developing ultrasound. Some were interested in producing detailed images of the inside of the body, while others attempted to use ultrasound to detect breast cancer or other tumors. A Scottish doctor named Ian Donald developed ultrasound for looking at the uterus (*see sidebar, below*).

Ultrasound for babies

At first, Donald investigated using ultrasound to detect cysts (fibrous growths) in ovaries. Then, in 1959, he noticed that the head of a fetus produced clear ultrasound readings, and he began using ultrasound to measure the heads of fetuses.

By 1966, the first ultrasound scanners were being produced commercially. The images were still poor quality, however. Ultrasound would perhaps not have caught on at all if it had not been for studies in the mid-1950s showing that exposure of a fetus to X-rays could cause leukemia (blood cancer) or other cancers. Ultrasound was regarded as a safe alternative to X-rays.

At present, ultrasound scans are used mainly to check on the developing fetus at various stages during pregnancy. Early in pregnancy, an ultrasound can reveal if a woman is carrying more than one fetus, which will help the woman and her doctor prepare for any special circumstances that may arise because of a multiple pregnancy.

Women usually have a second ultrasound scan at a later stage of their pregnancy. By that point, the fetus is often well developed,

CUTTING EDGE MOMENTS

Ultrasound to the rescue

In the 1950s, Ian Donald began experimenting with ultrasound. He used modified metal flaw detectors to see inside the body. Most doctors thought Donald's ideas would not work. In 1957, however, he used an ultrasound detector to examine a woman who doctors suspected had a tumor that was too advanced for surgery. With his machine, Donald found that the woman had an ovarian cyst, a growth on an ovary (a female reproductive organ) that is fairly easy to remove. Donald's diagnosis probably saved the woman's life. The case convinced many doctors that ultrasound was a useful medical tool.

and the sonographer (the technologist doing the scan) can often determine the sex of the fetus.

Additional ultrasounds are often performed on women considered "at risk pregnancies"—older women, those carrying a fetus that is smaller or larger than normal, or a woman carrying multiple fetuses.

Doctors also use ultrasound imaging during an amniocentesis procedure, which samples the amniotic fluid (the fluid surrounding the fetus in the uterus) using a hollow needle inserted into the uterus through the mother's abdomen. Amniocentesis reveals if a fetus has problems, including structural defects such as spina bifida (open spine), genetic problems such as Down syndrome, or if its lungs appear underdeveloped.

A pregnant woman having an ultrasound scan. The probe on the woman's abdomen sends out ultrasound waves and detects the echoes that return from inside the body. The fetus is clearly visible on the monitor.

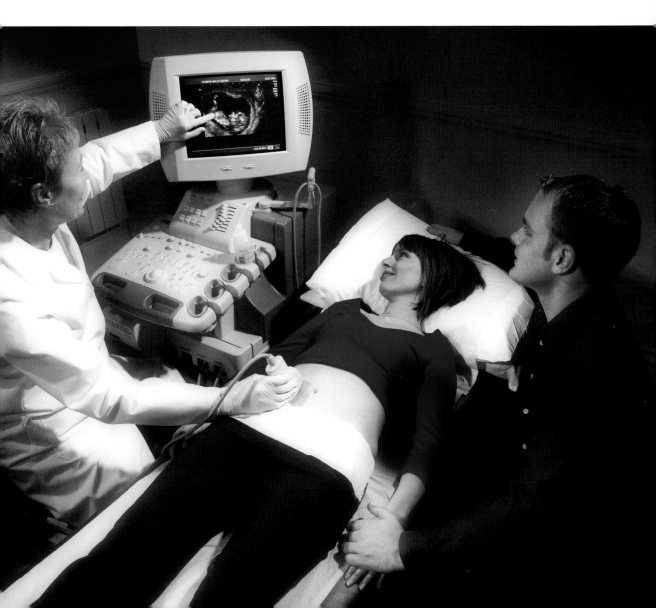

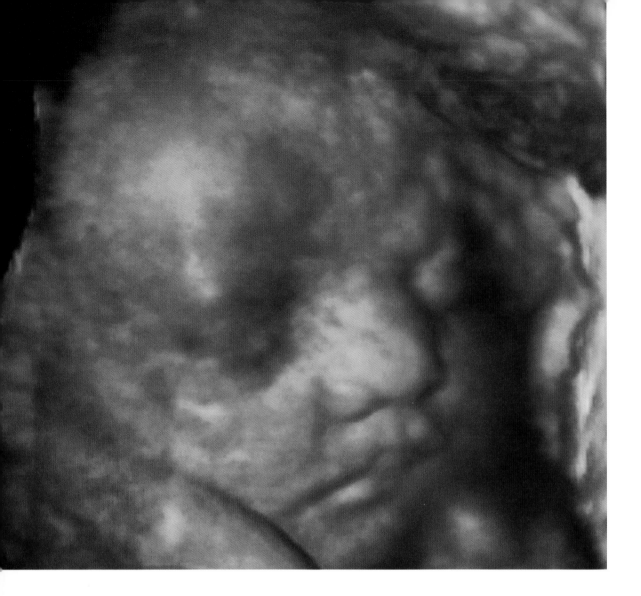

Doppler ultrasound

Another kind of ultrasound, known as Doppler ultrasound, was pioneered in 1955 by two Japanese scientists, Shigeo Satomura and Yasuhara Nimura. Doppler ultrasound uses the Doppler effect to tell whether blood is flowing toward or away from the ultrasound probe. The Doppler effect is the apparent change in the frequency, or pitch, of sound waves, depending on whether they are approaching or moving away from the observer. The Doppler effect is the reason that a siren on an ambulance sounds higher as it approaches and lower as it moves away. Doppler ultrasound picks up similar changes in the pitch of echoes coming back to the probe from flowing blood. If the echo is lower in pitch than the original signal, the blood is flowing away from the probe. If it is higher, the blood is flowing toward the probe.

Three-dimensional ultrasound techniques produce far more detailed images of the fetus than traditional ultrasound technology. This image, from the mid-1990s, is one of the earliest 3-D ultrasound images ever taken. It shows a developing fetus with a cleft lip—a genetic condition that can be treated with surgery.

During pregnancy, Doppler ultrasound can detect a fetal heartbeat many weeks before it can be heard by other methods, such as using a stethoscope. Doppler ultrasound is also used in general medicine to spot blockages in blood vessels and to diagnose diseases such as arteriosclerosis—a disorder, particularly of old age, in which the walls of the arteries (blood vessels carrying blood from the heart to the rest of the body) thicken and harden. Doppler ultrasound can also help diagnose cardiac (heart) valve problems. (Valves control blood flow through the heart's chambers.)

3-D ultrasound images

For three decades, researchers have been developing ultrasound scanners that could produce 3-D images. Ironically, the use of 3-D ultrasound imaging in medicine leaped ahead the most by borrowing technology from computer programs developed for the filmmaking industry. The same basic technology that makes animated films seem to "pop" from the screen now helps doctors diagnose problems in fetuses.

A normal ultrasound probe measures about 0.5 inch (1.2 centimeters) in diameter and contains sixty-four cables that produce the 2-D (two-dimensional) image. A 3-D ultrasound probe of the same diameter contains five hundred cables. This new probe attaches to instruments during laparoscopic (keyhole) surgery, which is performed using instruments inserted into the body through small incisions (cuts). Surgeons guide their instruments using the newly designed ultrasound probe, which produces sharp, 3-D ultrasound images of internal body structures.

CUTTING EDGE   SCIENCE

Ultrasound treatment

Ultrasound can be used to treat some medical problems instead of just diagnosing them. The vibrations in the tissues—and the warming that this produces—can help relieve many joint problems. Ultrasound is also a very effective treatment for kidney and bladder stones. Passing these hard lumps, which sometimes form in the kidney or bladder, can be very painful. In a procedure called lithotripsy, ultrasound breaks the stones into small pieces, which are then swept from body via blood or urine.

CHAPTER 7

Following the Traces

Different types of medical imaging are used for different purposes, depending on what the doctor wishes to see. Early X-rays, for instance, showed only bones, and could not be used to look at blood or soft tissues. Then, in 1910, researchers found a way of using X-rays to look at the intestines. They had a patient drink a radio-opaque liquid called a contrast medium, through which X-rays cannot pass. The contrast medium coated the intestines, which then showed up clearly on X-rays. In the 1920s, scientists found another contrast medium that could be safely injected into the bloodstream. This allowed doctors to take X-ray images of blood vessels in patients.

In an angiogram, a radio-opaque material (material through which X-rays cannot pass) is injected into the bloodstream to make the blood vessels show up. This angiogram shows the blood vessels of the heart.

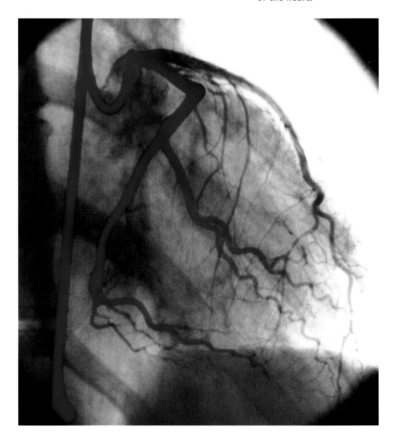

Early experiments

In January 1896, only weeks after Röentgen announced his discovery of X-rays, two Austrian doctors in Vienna took an X-ray of the blood vessels in the hand by injecting a compound of the chemical element mercury into the blood vessels of a cadaver (dead body). This technique could not be used on live patients because mercury is very poisonous.

By 1910, doctors discovered that they could safely give patients a compound made from the element bismuth to show the intestines on X-rays. Using this technique, doctors could find problems such as ulcers and perforations (holes) in the gut lining. Later, another element, barium, began to be used instead of bismuth.

In 1921, French doctor Jan Sicard accidentally discovered that an oily substance called lipidiol, known to be an effective painkiller, was also an excellent contrast medium. Lipidiol could be used to obtain good X-ray images of the spinal canal (the cavity down the middle of the spine that contains the spinal cord), the uterus, the bladder, and some joints. Lipidiol was not useful for X-raying the blood vessels, however.

X-raying the blood vessels

In the late 1920s, dyes containing the chemical element iodine were tested for use as contrast mediums in the blood. Some of these dyes were successful, and it was at last possible to produce angiograms

CUTTING EDGE   MOMENTS

X-raying the heart

In 1929, a young German hospital doctor, Werner Forssmann, began experimenting with a technique called catheterization. Practicing on cadavers, he figured out a way of inserting a narrow tube called a catheter into a blood vessel and feeding it through the blood vessel system to other areas of the body. He then injected a contrast medium into the blood through the catheter and took an X-ray. Forssmann was refused permission to try the experiment on a live patient, but he tried it anyway—on himself. While in his lab, he inserted a catheter 1 foot (30 cm) into a vein in his arm and injected contrast medium. Then, with the catheter still in place, he walked to the X-ray room and took an X-ray picture of the blood vessels in his arm as a document of the experiment. Forssmann was reprimanded for his experiment, but he had proved that the technique was safe. After World War II, other researchers used longer catheters to insert contrast medium into the heart, which made X-ray images of the heart possible. In 1956, Forssmann shared the Nobel Prize for Medicine with two other researchers for his pioneering work.

(X-rays showing the blood vessels) of living patients. In the late 1920s, this technique was adapted for studying blood flow through the heart.

Contrast mediums for scanners

As with conventional X-rays, images from CT scanners can be improved by the use of a contrast medium. Contrast mediums containing iodine highlight the blood vessels or the intestines.

A contrast medium is also sometimes useful in MRI scans. Most MRI contrast mediums contain the metal gadolinium. Gadolinium contrast mediums give very clear MRI images of the intestines, the liver, and the heart. A contrast medium can also be used for MRI scans of breast tissue if cancer is suspected. Once a cancerous tumor reaches a certain size, it develops its own blood supply. The contrast medium injected into the bloodstream can reveal the tumor through the extra network of blood vessels that form.

Pictures of the lungs

Lung tissue does not show up well in MRI scans. This occurs because the lungs are full of air, which does not have strong magnetic properties. A technique developed in the late 1990s by Professor Bill Hersman at the University of New Hampshire in Durham, New Hampshire, makes it possible to obtain very clear images of the lungs. In this technique, the patient breathes in a

CUTTING EDGE SCIENCE

Breast cancer screening

Breast cancer is one of the most common forms of cancer in women. In most developed countries, women fifty years of age and older are advised to have an annual checkup, called a mammogram, for signs of breast cancer. A mammogram is a detailed X-ray that helps detect early signs of cancer. Since the early 1990s, however, researchers have also been investigating the possibility of using MRI scans for breast cancer screening. MRI scans are clearer and show more details than X-rays, but the procedure takes longer and is much more expensive than a mammogram. Also, the extra detail in an MRI scan can occasionally lead to false positives—a diagnosis of cancer when, in fact, none exists.

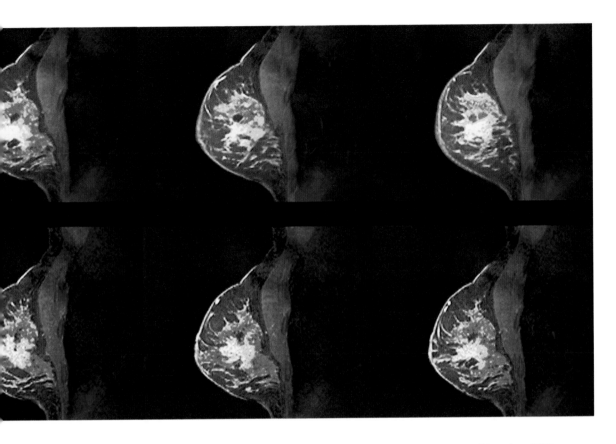

lungful of a special form of either helium or xenon gas. The patient holds the gas in his or her lungs for about ten seconds, during which time MRI scans are taken. Both of these gases give an MRI signal one hundred thousand times stronger than that of water, making possible very high-quality images of the lungs. The method is currently at an early research stage and is not used clinically. (It has not become an established medical procedure or treatment.)

This series of MRI scans shows several cross-sections through a woman's breast. The orange areas show the presence of breast cancer. A gadolinium contrast medium was used to make the cancer show up clearly.

Computer-enhanced images

The images from a CT or MRI scanner are created by a computer from a mass of data (information). The technologist, researcher, or doctor performing the procedure can program the computer to focus on one kind of information and not another. A CT or MRI scan can, therefore, be tailored to target the specific information needed for each patient. For instance, the person performing the test can program the computer to label particular tissues (say, tumors) with a certain bright color, while tissues that are not of interest can actually be removed from the image.

CHAPTER 8

Long, Thin Cameras

So far, all the techniques we have looked at involved indirect observation of the inside of the body. X-rays, sound waves, and other kinds of radiation all work by detecting the change in a signal directed at or passed into the body, from which a computer constructs an image. Since the 1960s, however, doctors have had another method available to them. It enables doctors or researchers to look directly into the body using nothing more complicated than a camera.

This endoscopic image of a stomach shows the wrinkled walls of the stomach. The many wrinkles allow the stomach to expand as it fills with food.

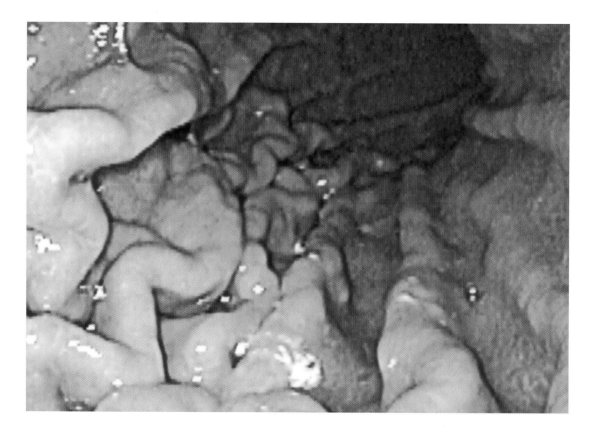

How an endoscope works

A flexible endoscope is made of bundles of fiber-optic cables that allow an inside view of the body. A light source is positioned outside the body and beamed through the cables. Lenses on the leading end of the cables focus the light. The endoscope can enter through the nose, mouth, rectum, or artificial opening to the body area being examined. As some of the optical fibers illuminate the inside of the body, others transmit an image back to a TV monitor. Endoscopes are named for the body area they explore, such as a gastroscope (for viewing the stomach), a bronchoscope (for viewing the lungs), or a colonoscope (for viewing the large intestine).

An endoscope is a tiny camera at the end of a long, thin, flexible tube. It is inserted into the body through a natural or artificially created opening to allow doctors to look inside the body. The tube of the endoscope is a fiber-optic cable—a bundle of hairlike glass fibers that transmit information in the form of pulses of light. Optic fibers also play an important role in transmitting telephone calls, connecting to the Internet, and broadcast media, such as TV and radio, around the globe. Despite their widespread use, however, optical fibers were developed for looking inside the body.

Early endoscopes

Tubelike instruments for looking into the body were developed in the nineteenth century, but until the invention of electric light, these devices were not very useful in the medical field. In 1910, Swedish doctor Hans Christian Jacobeus used a short, rigid endoscope to look inside a patient's chest. In 1912, he used a similar instrument to view a patient's abdomen (stomach area).

Endoscopic technology advanced significantly in 1957 when Basil Hirschowitz and colleagues developed a flexible endoscope, which could reach other body areas, and Lawrence Peters produced the first optical fibers. By the mid-1960s, endoscope use became widespread. In the 1980s, new, ultrathin "needlescopes" with cable diameters of less than 1 millimeter were developed. Ultrathin needlescopes allow doctors to examine blood vessels, heart valves, and the insides of eyeballs.

Ultrathin needlescopes contain thousands of pixels that provide a real-time image of previously inaccessible areas of the body. They easily view smaller body structures, such as the insides of the mammary glands in breast tissue.

Using endoscopes

Endoscopy helps diagnose many different medical problems. For example, flexible gastroscopes can be fed through the mouth and down the throat to examine the esophagus (the tube from the throat to the stomach) or to the stomach to look for bleeding, ulcers (sores in the stomach lining), or inflammation (swelling). A bronchoscope (also flexible) is fed through the mouth, down the trachea (windpipe), and into the lungs to look for evidence of bronchitis (inflammation of the airways), lung tumors, or infections. This test is also helpful for diagnosing adhesions—a condition in which the chest lining and the outer lining of the lungs stick together.

For other endoscope examinations, the endoscope is inserted through a small cut in the skin. For example, for joint surgeries, a type of endoscope called an arthroscope is inserted through a small cut to examine the knee or other joint. Unlike a gastroscope, an arthroscope is rigid and has a fairly short tube. It usually is not inserted far into the body. Doctors can also use an endoscope to look at abdominal organs, such as the intestines, liver, and gall bladder.

CUTTING EDGE   FACTS

Arthroscopic surgery

Until the 1990s, a patient who needed surgery on a knee or other joint spent several days in the hospital. Doctors usually made several large incisions (surgical cuts) to fix joint problems. Recovery often took weeks or months. Arthroscopic surgery—"keyhole" surgery of the joints—is much easier on a patient. It is usually done on an "outpatient" basis—the patient comes to the hospital for a few hours and goes home the same day. Recovery is quick and relatively easy. Knee surgery, for example, involves three tiny cuts: One for the arthroscope (so the surgeon can see), one for a cannula (a tube for pumping in saline), and one for surgical instruments. The saline makes the joint swell, which makes it easier for the doctor to see what he or she is doing and provides more room inside the body for the operation.

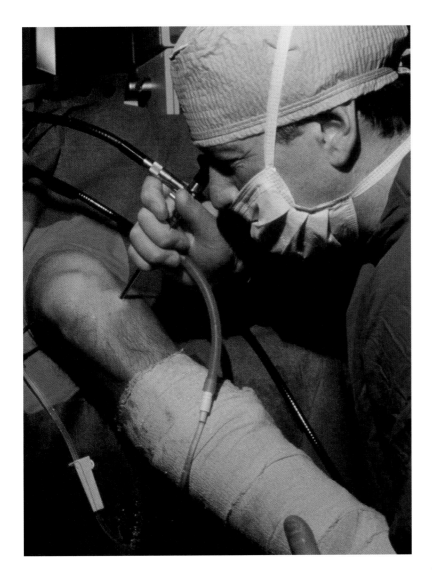

A surgeon uses an arthroscope to examine a patient's knee joint. The arthroscope is a steel tube containing optical fibers, a lens, and a light source. A scalpel or other surgical tool can be attached so that surgery can be done at the same time.

Not just for looking

Endoscopes are used for more than diagnosing problems. A number of surgical instruments can be attached to the end of an endoscope. For example, a scalpel on the end of the endoscope can take a biopsy (a small tissue sample) of a particular body organ or tumor.

Endoscopes are also useful during "keyhole surgery." The surgeon inserts specially designed cutting tools or other tiny surgical instruments through small incisions (cuts). Using the endoscope, the surgeon guides the instruments to the site of the injury or tumor and completes the operation without making a large incision in the patient's body.

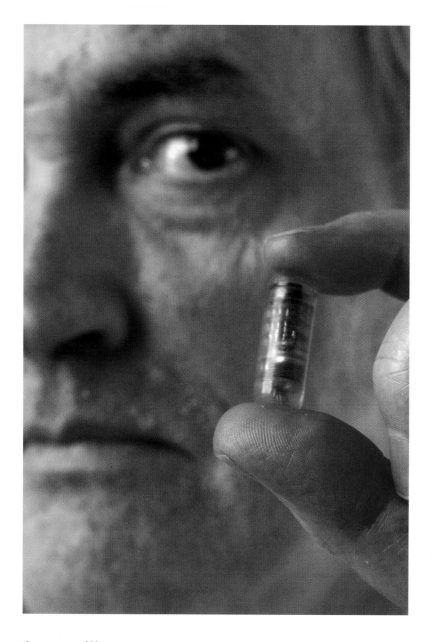

Professor Paul Swain, who led the team at the Royal London Hospital, in London, England, holds a capsule endoscope, or "camera in a pill." Swain's team of researchers developed the device. Just slightly longer than 1 inch (3.0 cm), the capsule endoscope is only a little larger than an ordinary pill. It also has a light source and a radio transmitter. Once it is swallowed, the patient cannot feel the pill, and can go about his or her day as normal. The endoscope is disposable and is flushed down the toilet after the patient passes it with other waste.

Camera pill

An endoscopy procedure allows the physician to inspect either the upper (from the throat to just below the stomach) or lower (the colon) digestive tract—but not the middle part of the digestive tract (the small intestine).

A wireless capsule endoscope, or the "camera in a pill," solves this problem. The capsule endoscope fits inside a pill swallowed by the patient. On its journey through the patient's intestinal tract, which lasts about eight hours, the camera takes as many as fifty thousand images. These images are transmitted to a wireless receiver worn by the patient. The doctor downloads the images and can watch a movie of the camera's trip through the patient's digestive tract.

The camera pill helps diagnose problems, such as bleeding in the small intestine, that cannot be diagnosed using other tests.

Robot cameras

Recent research has led to improvements in camera pills that make them even more effective. Doctors can control the newest versions —which are like tiny robots—by remote control. These robot cameras can be turned and even stopped as they move along the digestive tract, allowing the doctor to view areas of interest in the intestine wall. Tiny clamps on the capsule endoscopes allow the capsules to fix themselves to the wall of the intestine. Because the camera is anchored in one place, it does not get swept past an area the doctor wishes to study.

CUTTING EDGE   SCIENCE

Long-distance surgery

In June 2001, fourteen patients in a hospital in Rome, Italy, were examined by a surgeon who looked at their kidneys through an endoscope. The surgeon then performed a minor kidney operation on some of the patients. Operations of this sort are usually routine, but in this case, the surgeon was in Baltimore, Maryland. It was one of the first examples of telesurgery—in which a surgeon operates on a patient from a distance—in this case, from a different continent. Telesurgery uses a combination of video, medical imaging, and a remote-controlled robot to carry out the actual surgery. Using a robot this way is difficult at present, because the surgeon cannot feel what is going on—he or she can only see and hear the operation. Researchers are working on software that will allow the surgeon to "feel" what is happening during the operation as well as see it.

CHAPTER 9

Combining Techniques

Each type of medical imaging has advantages and disadvantages. The key factors involved in evaluating the pros and cons of different techniques include versatility and availability, cost, and potential side effects.

CT scanners provide quality images quickly, especially for harder tissues. CT involves the use of X-rays, which can harm the body in large doses and cannot be used at all on pregnant women.

PET scans show information about tissue function (for instance the uptake of glucose) instead of their structure. PET also uses radioactive materials, so the cautions stated above apply.

MRI scans are clear and detailed. MRI does not use radiation to produce images; however, high-quality MRI scans are slow and expensive. MRI cannot be used on patients who have metal implants or pacemakers, and it does not show bones or the lungs. Also, many patients experience feelings of claustrophobia (fear of enclosed spaces) during MRI scans. Certain medical centers also have "open MRI" machines that do not fully enclose a patient, which lessens the feeling of claustrophobia. A specialized MRI procedure called functional MRI (fMRI) shows the processes going on inside the body. fMRI involves making a background scan of a body organ or tissue, to which an active scan of the same area is compared.

Ultrasound is safer than other techniques, which is why it is used during pregnancy. Conventional ultrasound scans are cheaper than other kinds of scan, but give poor-quality images. High-quality 3-D ultrasound scans are considerably more expensive.

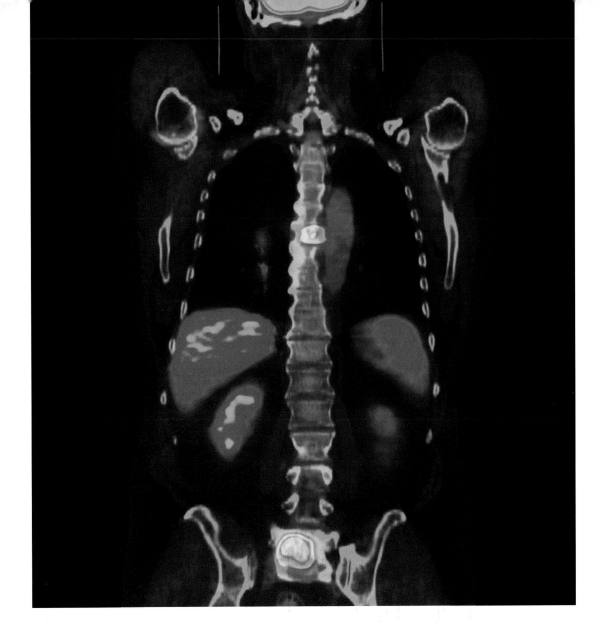

Imaging tumors

One important use of medical imaging is for detecting tumors as early as possible. Early tumors do not show up clearly on CT scans because the cancerous tissue does not look different from surrounding tissues. A PET scan reveals early tumors because it picks up the faster oxygen uptake of rapidly dividing cancer cells. PET scans do not, however, show much structural detail. A combination of a PET scan with a CT scan clearly detects early tumors and reveals enough structural details to pinpoint the location of the tumor.

This image uses a combination of PET and CT to show the locations of a number of tumors in a patient with cancer of the nervous system. Green, yellow, and red areas indicate tumors. Normal bone is blue.

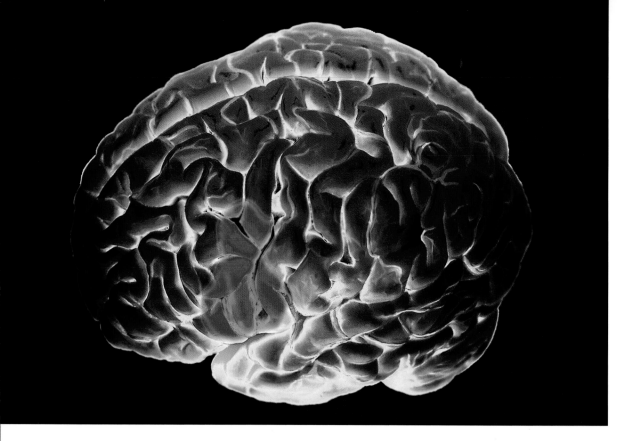

Endoscopy is also a safe technique that provides high-quality images. Endoscopes can only look at a small area of the body in each image and cannot see through bone or tissue.

In the early twenty-first century, as the use of various kinds of scanners have become more widespread and available, researchers and doctors have discovered the advantages of combining different imaging techniques. This practice compensates for any disadvantages of using only one type of scanner and improves the accuracy of diagnoses.

This image combines a 3-D MRI scan of the whole brain with a PET scan that shows brain activity when the patient is asked to perform a particular task. In this case, the scan shows the brain area that is most active when the patient thinks about specific words.

Improved brain images

Combined scans are useful for looking at the brain. Normal MRI scans show the structures of the brain in great detail, but they are slow and do not give any information about brain activity. fMRI scans show blood flow in the brain, indicating which parts of the brain are most active. They can also be done several times per second. PET scans are also fast and can show brain activity. Alternatively, PET scans can be tailored to show different types of nerve connections in the brain. A combination of MRI with PET or fMRI scans provides good images of the structures of the brain as well as information about which parts are active.

Combined brain scans are used mainly for brain research, but are increasingly used to reveal abnormal activity patterns that indicate illnesses affecting the brain. Combined MRI/PET scans are also important in research into new drugs.

Spotting fast changes

One problem with images of the brain is that nerve activity in the brain changes or disappears within a few milliseconds. Even fMRI and PET cannot keep track of changes that occur at this speed.

Two techniques that can detect such rapid changes are EEGs (electroencephalograms) and MEGs (magnetoencephalograms). EEGs monitor electrical activity in the brain. For an EEG, the doctor places several electrodes (conductors of electricity) on the patient's head. The electrodes pick up the electrical activity of nerve impulses traveling through the brain. MEGs are similar, but measure changes in magnetism instead of electrical activity. Both techniques show changes in real time and give researchers only a vague idea of the location of brain activity. By combining EEGs and MEGs with brain imaging, however, researchers can pinpoint exactly where moment-by-moment changes occur.

CUTTING EDGE   SCIENCE

PET in drug research

A combination of PET with MRI or CT is proving enormously useful in research into new drugs. Companies developing new drugs have been using PET for some time to test the effects of new drugs on animals. The drug being tested is radioactively tagged and PET scans can show the path of the drug through the body.

Now researchers are also using PET, combined with MRI or CT, to directly test the effectiveness of some drugs on humans. For instance, a protein called amyloid forms plaques in the brain in people who have Alzheimer's disease (a disorder that affects the brain, especially late in life). Researchers have found a substance that binds to amyloid in the brain, and this substance can be given a radioactive tag. Researchers can then use PET to directly test for amyloid levels in the brains of patients with Alzheimer's. This test is also very useful for checking the effectiveness of drugs that treat Alzheimer's by lowering amyloid levels. PET scans performed before and after administration of the drug help measure any changes in amyloid levels.

CHAPTER 10

Not Just For Diagnostic Purposes

We saw in Chapter 8 that endoscopes can be used in keyhole surgery as well as for diagnosing illnesses. Today, other kinds of medical imaging are being used in surgery and to help focus on specific body areas during treatment.

Killing off tumors

Radiation therapy has been used as a treatment for some kinds of cancer for many years. Radiation is dangerous to humans because it damages dividing cells, but it is also useful to doctors for the same reason. Cancer cells divide rapidly, so radiation damages cancer cells more than it damages other body tissues. By giving a patient a short, focused dose of gamma rays or X-rays, doctors can use radiation to control or kill tumors. Radiation has been used for this purpose since the early twentieth century.

CUTTING EDGE MOMENTS

MRI lifts depression

A surprising discovery in 2004 suggests that MRI may have other uses besides imaging. Researchers looking at the brains of depressed patients discovered that after having MRI brain scans, patients with certain kinds of depression were much happier. This improvement in mood lasted for some time. The combination of electrical and magnetic fields produced during MRI scans seem to have worked in some unknown way to lift depression—with no side effects. MRI scans are very expensive, so researchers are now doing animal tests on a smaller, simpler device that produces similar electric and magnetic fields. This kind of magnetic therapy may eventually become a common treatment for depression.

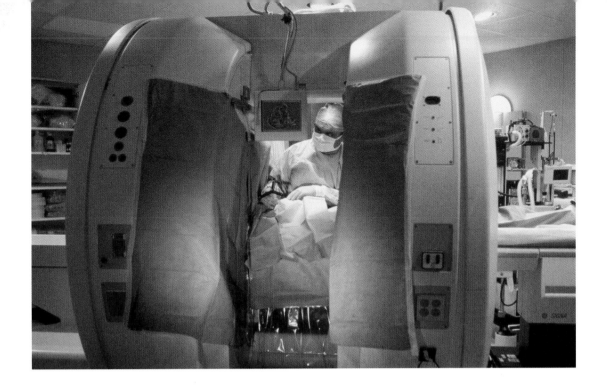

Radiation therapy often has unpleasant side effects such as hair loss and nausea. Radiation therapy is also not always successful. If the radiation therapy can be more accurately targeted on the cancer site, treatment is more likely to be successful with less chance of unpleasant side effects. Modern PET, MRI, or CT scanners can help focus radiation very accurately on particular areas of the body. High-quality 3-D images of the cancer tissue enable doctors to see exactly where to aim the radiation. The therapy becomes more effective and less radiation is needed to destroy the tumor.

A surgeon performs a brain operation on a patient in an open-sided MRI scanner. The surgeon uses a 3-D image of the brain (shown in dark blue on the monitor) to guide his instruments. During the surgery, continous new scans keep the surgeon aware of what is occurring inside the brain.

Guiding surgery

Since the late 1990s, advances in MRI scanners and computer software have made it possible for surgeons to perform brain operations that would be almost impossible otherwise. Sometimes brain tumors develop very close to vital areas of the brain, such as those that control movement or speech. A tiny error by the surgeon could leave the patient paralyzed or unable to talk. MRI plays an important role in instances such as these.

Surgeons first take a high-quality, 3-D MRI image of the brain. If the problem is a tumor, the MRI scan is combined with a PET or fMRI image showing the position of the tumor. Another MRI or CT scan may be required to show the position of important blood vessels or other structures that the surgeon needs to see clearly when carrying out the operation.

When the surgeon begins the operation, a TV monitor in the operating room shows the MRI image superimposed on a live video of the patient's head. Sophisticated computer software exactly aligns the laser scanner and the actual head (*see sidebar, below*). This technique allows the surgeon to track the minute changes that may occur during the operation.

Tracking the scalpel

As the operation progresses, tissues within the skull may move somewhat. Consequently, when the surgeon cuts into the brain, he or she might not find the tumor in exactly the same place as indicated by the original MRI image. To overcome this problem, the surgeon performs the operation in an advanced MRI scanner that has an open section in the middle where he or she can stand. During the operation, the surgeon takes additional MRI scans to see if there are any changes in the position of the tumor or other tissues. The surgeon who works inside the MRI scanner must use specially designed, non-magnetic surgical instruments.

Surgery using MRI imaging is currently used mainly for brain operations. The technique may soon be used in other operations, for instance, to assist in complex operations on bones, the kidneys, the liver, and the spine.

CUTTING EDGE   SCIENCE

Connecting images with lasers

For surgery, MRI scans are precisely aligned with live video images using a laser scanner. A laser (short for Light Amplification by Stimulated Emission of Radiation) is a device that produces a highly focused, narrow light beam. The laser scanner moves a beam of laser light rapidly backward and forward over the patient's head, measuring the distance from the scanner to the head at each point. The measurements are passed to a computer, which creates a "map" of the contours of the head. The computer also contains a previously recorded MRI scan with a detailed model of the patient's head. The computer compares the contours of the laser map with the contours of the MRI model and rotates the model until it aligns exactly with the laser scan. Changes in the position of the head are detected by the laser scanner, and the MRI scan is aligned with the head movements.

Opposite: Here is what the surgeon shown on page 51 might see while performing open-sided MRI brain surgery. The image shows the position of the brain tumor (green) that is the reason for the surgery, as well as major blood vessels around the tumor (purple).

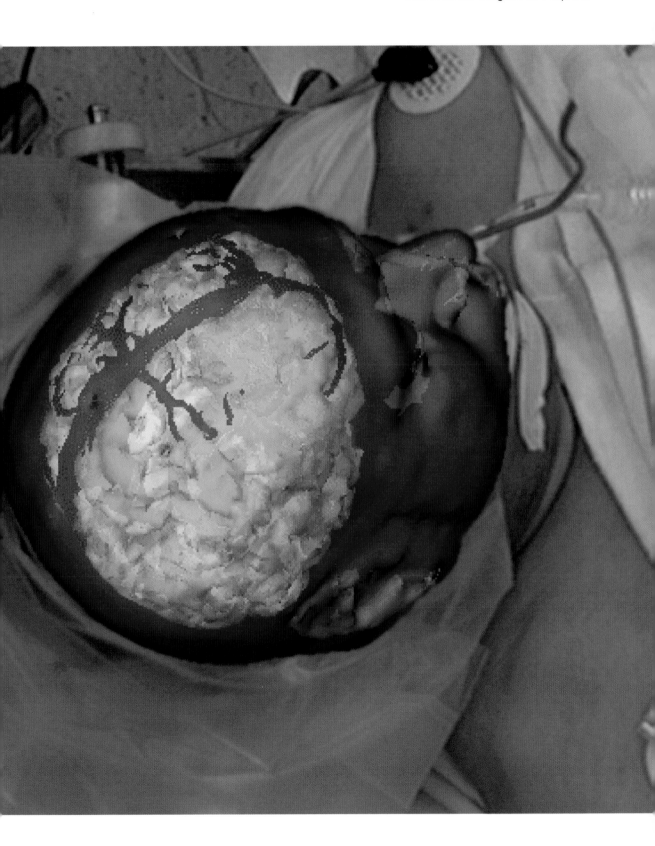

CHAPTER 11

Future Technologies

Imagine this scene: A man has been hit by a bus and is seriously injured. A bystander calls an ambulance, which arrives within a few minutes. Although the victim does not have obvious injuries, he is in great pain. One of the emergency medical team members uses a small magnetic device to switch off the pain centers in the injured man's brain. Another emergency team member pulls out a handheld scanner and passes it over the patient's body. The scanner pinpoints the major areas of injury.

The ambulance team sends the images to a hospital, where they are passed to the emergency room physician. He or she alerts the surgeon who will need to operate on the patient, and the surgeon immediately begins preparing for the operation. Once at the hospital, the surgeon repairs bleeding in the man's brain using keyhole surgery. She makes a small hole in the skull and inserts a tiny, remote-controlled "robot surgeon." The robot stops the bleeding with a tiny laser.

CUTTING EDGE   SCIENCE

TMS

TMS (transcranial magnetic stimulation) is a recently developed method for magnetically stimulating the brain. It may have potential as a treatment for depression. A pulse of magnetism from a TMS device can either stimulate part of the brain or briefly turn it off. TMS is being used in brain research, in combination with PET or fMRI imaging, to observe how magnetic stimulation affects brain activity. In addition to its possible use in the treatment of depression, TMS might also be used to temporarily "knock out" the pain centers of the brain for effective and safe pain relief.

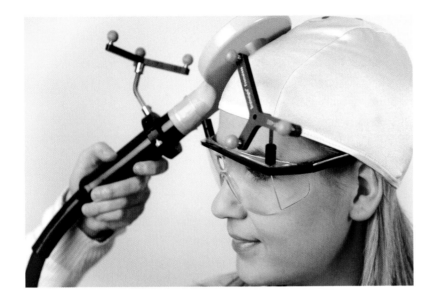

TMS equipment is being used here to map the brain. TMS stimulates specific brain areas, and the effects of the stimulation on the patient are recorded. By stimulating different brain areas, physicians can map stimulation effects.

The previous scenario could not happen today, but it could occur in the near future. Medical imaging has made incredible strides since the first X-rays were made in 1896. The pace of change of future improvements in technology will occur even faster. Thirty years from now, scanners will have changed beyond recognition.

Problems solved

Improvements to current scanners will soon be available. CT scanners that use two detectors with a single X-ray tube should scan twice as quickly as single-detector machines and provide better images with smaller doses of X-rays.

Open-sided MRI scanners are already in use, and new machines are being developed that can produce even better images. But an even more useful way of improving MRI scanners would be to make them smaller and cheaper. In 2004, two U.S. researchers made important improvements to a very sensitive magnetic detector called an atomic magnetometer. This technology is far more sensitive than the detectors currently used in MRI scanners, and would be much smaller, lighter, and cheaper.

HUTT

Although existing scanners will continue to improve, a new kind of ultrasound scan known as high-resolution ultrasonic transmission tomography (HUTT) could prove itself superior to all the existing techniques. Conventional ultrasound scanners work by detecting the echoes of ultrasound pulses fired into the body. During an ultrasound scan, two thousand times as many sound waves pass through the body as bounce back as echoes. HUTT not only detects sound waves that pass through the body, but also detects how they have changed. HUTT scanners can therefore produce images with much greater resolution (clarity) and detail than conventional ultrasound scans, including those taken with the latest 3-D technology. Images produced by HUTT scanning are even better than those obtained from CT or MRI scanners.

HUTT scanners can also differentiate between different kinds of body tissue. As the ultrasound pulses pass through the body's tissues, each pulse changes in different ways. Detectors can pick up these differences, and a computer uses that information to distinguish between the tissues.

Seeing with light

Optical imaging—scanning the body using light—is another promising new technique. Ordinary light does not pass through the

CUTTING EDGE   SCIENCE

Seeing our thoughts?

In the future, will we be able to use imaging techniques to read people's thoughts? Using imaging combinations such as MRI and PET, scientists are already finding patterns of brain activity that may offer clues about what a person is thinking. As researchers obtain clearer images of these patterns and get better at interpreting their meanings, it may become possible to read someone's thoughts from a brain scan. Some scientists are sceptical about this, however. They cite experiments that suggest there are no consistent patterns in brain activity and that people thinking about similar things can display very different brain patterns.

body. If it did, we would be transparent! Some kinds of infrared light (long wavelengths of electromagnetic radiation) are not absorbed by the body's tissues and pass right through the body. Researchers are now developing imaging methods that shine

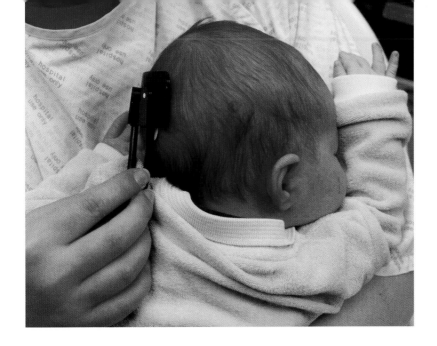

A handheld optical imaging scanner is used to check a baby's brain. Optical imaging is useful here because babies are vulnerable to damage from X-rays. CT scanning cannot be used on infants. MRI is unsatisfactory because a baby cannot remain still for the time needed to do an MRI scan.

infrared light though the body and then measure how the light is changed by its passage through the body. As with HUTT, the infrared wavelengths may create images of the inside of the body.

Research carried out into the use of optical imaging for breast screening suggests that this technique could detect breast cancer earlier than any other imaging technique. Current optical imaging scanners can only penetrate about 6 inches (15 centimeters) beneath the skin. This is deep enough for breast screening, but it limits other uses of the technique.

Imaging in surgery

As medical imaging techniques become faster, they will almost certainly become an essential part of surgery. Surgeons wearing virtual reality (VR) goggles will be able to see scans of the patient taken in real time, superimposed over video images of the patient's exterior. Through their VR goggles, surgeons will see markers indicating the exact positions of their surgical instruments as well as the area of the body they are targeting. As we saw in Chapter 10, much of this is already possible.

Tiny robots

Improvements in the camera pill described on pages 44 and 45 will soon revolutionize endoscopy. Instead of flexible tubes, doctors will introduce tiny robot cameras into the body, which will increase the comfort level of such tests for patients. In 2004, a U.S. research team developed a robot camera that is about the size of an adult's thumb. The tiny camera can be inserted into a patient's abdomen. Once in place, doctors can move the robot by remote control. Such robots will give a doctor "eyes" inside a patient's body. Members of an emergency medical team at the scene of an accident could put a robot camera into a person's body, and doctors at the local hospital could use the images to plan the best course of treatment for the patient. If sufficiently small robots are developed, it might even be possible to inject them directly into the bloodstream. Such robots could be used, for instance, to clear the kinds of blood clots that cause heart attacks and some kinds of stroke.

An exciting future

The discovery of X-rays fired the imagination of the whole world. For the first time, people could look inside a living body without cutting it open. Today, images of the inside of the body are commonplace and of far higher quality than Wilhelm Röentgen could have ever dreamed. The current scanners that produce these pictures are large and expensive, and may soon be replaced by smaller, cheaper, and more powerful models. The science of medical imaging is rapidly developing and changing, and new, more sophisticated techniques for seeing inside the body are being invented constantly. Handheld scanners, microrobots, and virtual reality surgery are just some of the possibilities that could improve diagnostic techniques as well as treatments for disease or trauma in the not-too-distant future.

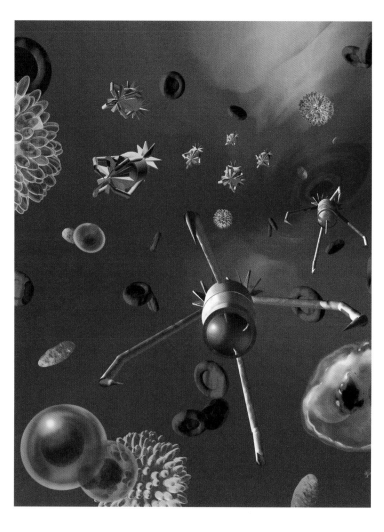

An artist's impression of microscopic medical robots at work in the human body. We may soon be able to make devices that can travel through blood vessels and other parts of the body. One type could carry a camera and other medical imaging equipment. Another could carry tiny surgical tools or drugs to treat any problems they encounter.

CUTTING EDGE FACTS

Milestones in medical imaging

Date	Event
1895	Wilhelm Röentgen discovers X-rays.
1896	Thomas Edison demonstrates the fluoroscope.
1904	Clarence Dally, Edison's assistant, dies from X-ray burns.
1910	Hans Christian Jacobeus uses a rigid endoscope to look inside the chest.
1913	The Bucky grid and the Coolidge tube greatly improve X-ray quality.
1921	Jan Sicard and Jacques Forestier first use lipidiol as a contrast medium.
1928	S. Y. Sokolov makes the first ultrasound fault detector.
1931	International agreement is reached on a maximum safe X-ray dose.
1934	George Hevesy uses the first radioactive tracer.
1937	Karl and Friedrich Dussik obtain crude ultrasound images of the brain.
1946	Edward Purcell and Felix Bloch develop NMR.
1949–1951	Early ultrasound research is conducted in the U.S.
1955	The image intensifier makes it possible to look at X-rays on a TV screen.
1957	Basil Hirschowitz and colleagues develop the first flexible endoscope.
1959	Ian Donald first uses ultrasound on pregnant women.
1968	The first SPECT machines are introduced.
1970–1977	Early work is carried out on MRI by Raymond Damadian and Paul Lauterbur.
1971	The first CT scanner is demonstrated by Godfrey Hounsfield.
1975	The first PET machines are built. Improved ultrasound machines become widespread.
1977	Damadian demonstrates the first whole-body MRI scanner.
Early 1980s	The first commercial MRI scanners become available.
1990	Seiji Ogawa and colleagues demonstrate fMRI.
2001	Commercial 3-D ultrasound machines become available. The first camera pill is developed.
2005	The first demonstrations of HUTT.

Glossary

abdomen The stomach area of the body.

Alzheimer's disease A progressive brain disorder that causes memory loss and an eventual inability to read, write, or speak.

angiography The process of taking X-ray images of the blood vessels by injecting a contrast medium (a liquid opaque to X-rays) into the bloodstream.

arteriosclerosis A condition in which the walls of the arteries (blood vessels carrying blood from the heart to the rest of the body) thicken and harden.

atoms The fundamental particles from which all substances are composed.

bronchoscope A type of endoscope that is used to examine the lungs.

cancer An disease in which a group or groups of cells begin to grow uncontrollably.

cartilage A strong, springy kind of tissue that forms some parts of the nose, ears, skeleton, and joints.

catheter A thin, flexible tube that can be inserted into a blood vessel or other part of the body to inject or drain off fluids.

cathode ray tube A glass tube with the air pumped out of it, containing two electrodes that allow electricity to pass through the tube.

colon The large intestine.

cyclotron A large machine used for studying atoms and subatomic particles. Radioisotopes are made in cyclotrons.

cyst An abnormal sac, often filled with fluid or fibrous material, that develops inside the body.

diagnosis The identification of an illness or disorder in a patient.

electromagnetic spectrum The different wavelengths of mostly invisible energy waves (radiation) that travel at the speed of light; includes visible light, X-rays, radio waves, microwaves, infrared (heat) radiation, and gamma rays.

endoscope A thin, often flexible tube with a lighted lens at one end that is used to look inside the body.

endoscopy The practice of looking into the body and/or performing surgery using an endoscope.

epilepsy A disorder of the nervous system in which the patient sometimes has bouts of uncontrollable movements or unconsciousness.

fetus A developing unborn child more than eight weeks old.

fluorescent A material that glows when light or some other kind of radiation hits it.

gamma rays Very high-energy, dangerous electromagnetic radiation produced by some radioactive substances.

Geiger counter An instrument for detecting and measuring radioactivity.

glucose A sugar that is the main fuel used by cells to produce the energy they need to work and grow.

HUTT (high-resolution ultrasonic transmission tomography) a type of ultrasound scanner that detects the changes in sound waves as they pass through the body; HUTT produces images of exceptional detail and clarity.

incision A cut made by a surgeon during an operation.

inflammation A swelling of a joint or other body part.

intestine The long digestive tube between the stomach and the anus.

keyhole surgery Surgery performed using endoscopes inserted through small incisions in the body (*see laparoscopy*).

laparoscopy The use of an endoscope to look at and/or perform surgery through small openings cut in the body (*see keyhole surgery*).

laser A device that produces a highly focused, pure beam of light.

leukemia A kind of blood cancer that affects the white blood cells.

multiple sclerosis A disease that causes gradual, worsening damage to the nervous system.

optical fibers Flexible fibers made from glass that conduct light pulses along their length.

organ A part of the body with a particular function, such as the heart, liver, or stomach.

pacemaker An electrical device inserted under the skin that helps regulate the heartbeat.

paralyzed Unable to move all or part of the body.

pituitary gland A small organ in the brain that produces chemicals that circulate in the blood and controls the actions of hormones in the body.

positron An incredibly small particle, similar to an electron, but with a positive electric charge. An electron is an extremely small particle that orbits the nucleus of an atom. It has almost no mass but carries a negative electrical charge.

radiation Waves or rays of energy, such as visible light, X-rays, radio waves, and infrared waves.

radioactive A substance that emits (produces) ionizing (dangerous) radiation.

radioisotope The form of an element that is radioactive.

radiology The study of X-rays and other kinds of high-energy radiation; may also refer to the department of a hospital that uses X-rays and other radiation to diagnose or treat diseases.

telesurgery Surgery performed by remote control from another location.

tissue A part of the body made from cells that are all similar. Muscle, bone, and skin are types of tissue.

tomography The technique of making images of slices through the body.

tumor An abnormal growth in the body. Some tumors are benign—they often stop growing after a short time and remain in one place in the body. Malignant tumors invade surrounding tissues and spread to other organs, causing illnesses, disabilities, and even death.

ulcer A sore patch in the body caused by a break in the skin or a membrane.

ultrasound Very high-pitched sounds above the frequency range of human hearing.

vacuum Completely empty space, without air or other gases in it.

voxels Small blocks that make up a 3-D computer image. Voxels are similar to the pixels (the individual tiny dots) that make up a flat computer image.

Further Information

BOOKS

Kevles, Bettyann Holzmann. *Naked to the Bone: Medical Imaging in the Twentieth Century.* Perseus (1998).

McClafferty, Carla Killough. *Something Out of Nothing: Marie Curie and Radium.* Farrar, Straus and Giroux (BYR) (2006).

McClafferty, Carla Killough. *The Head Bone's Connected To The Neck Bone: The Weird, Wacky, and Wonderful X-Ray.* Farrar, Straus and Giroux (BYR) (2001).

Santella, Andrew. *Marie Curie.* Trailblazers of the Modern World (series). World Almanac® Library (2001).

Wolbarst, Anthony Brinton. *Looking Within: How X-Ray, CT, MRI, Ultrasound,and Other Medical Image Are Created, and How They Help Physicians Save Lives.* University of California Press (1999).

Woolf, Alex. *History of Medicine: Medicine in the Twentieth Century and Beyond.* Enchanted Lion Books (2006).

WEB SITES

imaginis.com/faq/history.asp
Explore an overview of the history of medical imaging and follow links included in the time line of medical imaging for more information.

www.fda.gov/cdrh/ct/what.html
Visit the U.S. Food and Drug Administration's Web site about computed tomagraphy and explore the many links that offer more details.

nobelprize.org/medicine/laureates/1979/ hounsfield-autobio.html
Read a short autobiography of Godfrey Hounsfield, the man who invented CT.

imagers.gsfc.nasa.gov/ems/ems.html
Discover more information about electromagnetic radiation and the electromagnetic spectrum.

faculty.washington.edu/chudler/image.html
Find out about the different technologies doctors use to look inside your brain.

Index

Index *(continued)*